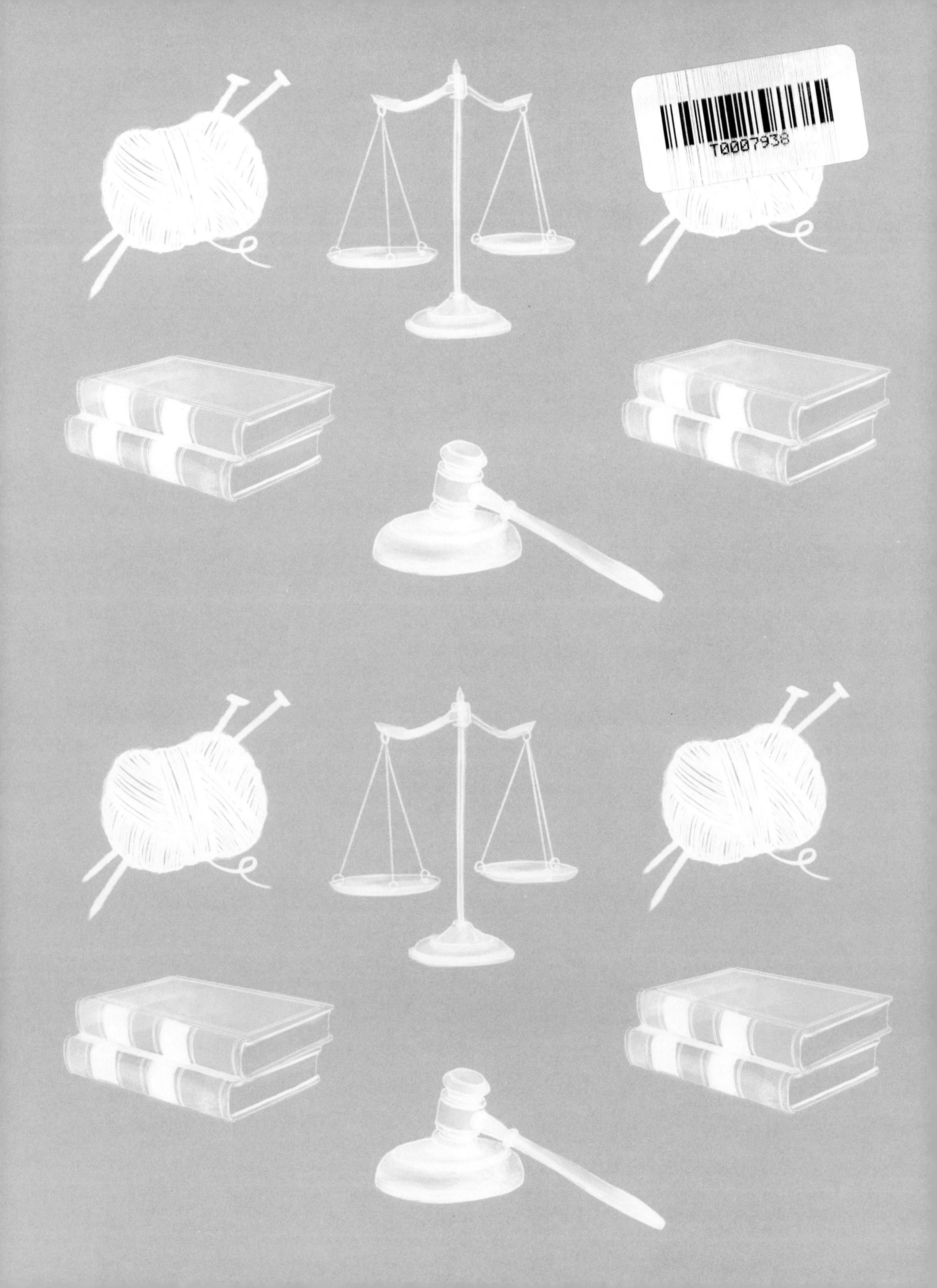

JUSTICE KETANJI

The Story of US Supreme Court Justice

KETANJI BROWN JACKSON

Library of Congress Cataloging-in-Publication Data available

ISBN 978-1-338-88529-3

10 9 8 7 6 5 4 3 2 1 23 24 25 26 27

Printed in China 38

First edition, August 2023

Book design by Rae Crawford

JUSTICE KETANJI

The Story of US Supreme Court Justice KETANJI BROWN JACKSON

Written by Denise Lewis Patrick

Illustrated by Kim Holt

ORCHARD BOOKS
New York
an imprint of Scholastic Inc.

On a warm Florida afternoon, four-year-old Ketanji Onyika Brown was waiting for her father to come home from his classes. When he took out his law books to study, Ketanji took out her coloring books.

Ketanji's parents, grandparents, and their parents before them all worked hard to make a good life for their family. Her parents had both been public school teachers.

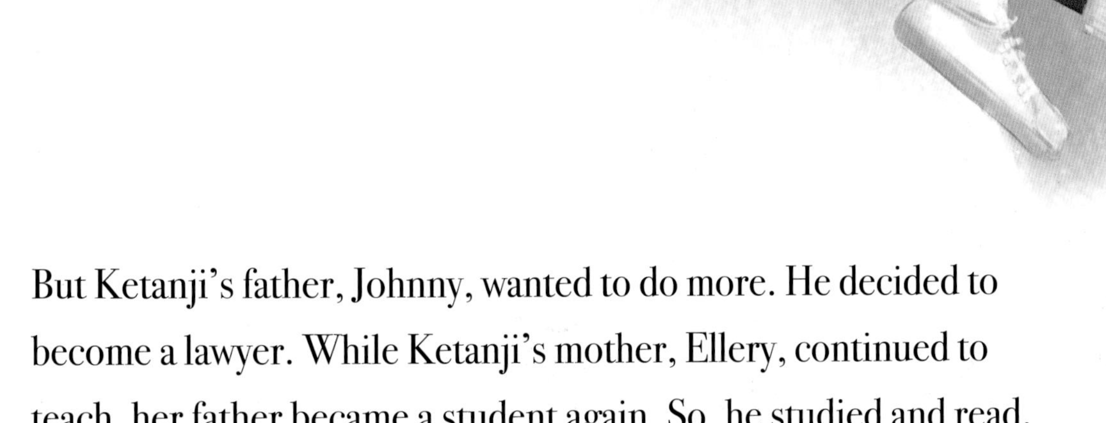

But Ketanji's father, Johnny, wanted to do more. He decided to become a lawyer. While Ketanji's mother, Ellery, continued to teach, her father became a student again. So, he studied and read. Ketanji watched and listened.

"You can do anything. You can be anything," he told his bright-eyed brown daughter.

She remembered.

Senior Class Officers

President Ketanji Brown

Soon, words were part of Ketanji's world, too. She loved reading them. She loved writing them. Most of all, she loved speaking them. When she started Miami Palmetto High School, she joined the speech and debate team and found friends who also loved words.

Ketanji's sharp thinking and crisp, clear voice helped the team win many competitions. Her sure way of speaking stood out so much that her classmates voted her to be class president.

Ketanji always knew she would attend college after high school, and she aimed for one of the best: Harvard University in Cambridge, Massachusetts.

Her school counselor told her, “You shouldn’t set your sights so high.”

But Ketanji remembered: *You can do anything.*

She worked hard. She applied to Harvard, and she was accepted.

HARVARD

At Harvard, Ketanji began to meet new people. Her roommates became her friends, and as time passed she began to call those friends her sisters. But once again, some people made her feel like she didn't belong. She spoke out – and proved that she *did* belong, by attending protests and keeping up with her classes at the same time.

Brilliant, bright-eyed Ketanji Brown graduated from Harvard with special honors. One year later, she set her mind to work again and followed her father's footsteps to attend Harvard Law School.

The year she completed Harvard Law School, she married Patrick Graves Jackson. Then she began to set her sights even higher on jobs at top law firms. *You can be anything!* she believed. She entered a new world, full of more challenges and surprises.

Ketanji Brown Jackson practiced many types of law. She joined law firms, both big and small. She worked as a clerk to three different judges, including Justice Stephen Breyer of the US Supreme Court. She defended poor people in court.

While working and having a family, she thought about the women who made her feel strong, like her mother, her aunt, and her grandmother. She thought about another woman who inspired her, the trailblazer Constance Baker Motley. Motley was the first Black woman to become a US district judge. (US district judges look at facts and laws to solve disagreements about who's right in a legal case.)

After seventeen years in law, Ketanji was nominated to become a US district judge herself. A group of US senators had to question her first. At breaks during their meetings, Ketanji used her knitting to keep calm. By then, she was known and respected for her words and her sharp thinking about the law. The senators voted her in.

Years later, President Joe Biden decided that Judge Ketanji Brown Jackson had the skills and experience to serve on the highest court in the country – the United States Supreme Court. He nominated her to replace retiring justice Stephen Breyer.

Again, Judge Jackson faced four days of meetings with senators. They asked her about everything from her time at Harvard to her past jobs to her feelings about various laws. Though many supported her, some just didn't think she belonged. Ketanji didn't protest. She knew how hard she'd worked, and how much she'd learned in her career.

She didn't need to knit scarves to answer with calmness and grace. Behind her each day sat her parents, Johnny and Ellery; her brother, Ketajh; her husband, Patrick; her daughters, Talia and Leila; and her sister-friends. And in her mind were her grandparents and their parents before them.

SEAL OF THE PRESIDENT OF THE UNITED STATES

Finally, in a vote of 53 to 47, Judge Ketanji Brown Jackson was confirmed as the 116th United States Supreme Court justice. She became the first Black woman to sit on the court in its 232-year history.

She remembered.

She believed.

She knew.

You can do anything.

You can be anything.

BIBLIOGRAPHY

Anderson, Jessica, and The Associated Press. "Biden's Supreme Court nominee Ketanji Brown Jackson has a Baltimore connection: Her brother once worked for the Baltimore Police." *Baltimore Sun.* https://www.baltimoresun.com/maryland/baltimore-city/bs-md-ci-ketanji-brown-jackson-20220225-stynon4wlrduripxqk5tffefam-story.html.

Baker, Shamonee. "Uncles of Ketanji Brown Jackson applaud her Supreme Court nomination from Tallahassee." *Tallahassee Democrat.* https://www.tallahassee.com/story/news/2022/03/28/kentaji-brown-jackson-supreme-court-tallahassee-famu-calvin-ross-uncles-family-nomination-hearing/7155513001/.

Blanco, Adrian, and Shelly Tan. "How Ketanji Brown Jackson's path to the Supreme Court differs from the current justices." *Washington Post.* https://www.washingtonpost.com/politics/interactive/2022/ketanji-brown-jackson-school-career/.

Chilton, Charlotte. "42 Photos of Miami During the Iconic 1980s." *Esquire.* https://www.esquire.com/lifestyle/g29664917/best-miami-1980s-photos/.

Cowan, Jill, Patricia Mazzei, and Tariro Mzezewa. "How Black Women Saw Ketanji Brown Jackson's Confirmation Hearing." *New York Times.* https://www.nytimes.com/2022/03/25/us/ketanji-brown-jackson-black-women.html?searchResultPosition=14.

Creamer, Ella. "55 Things You Need to Know About Ketanji Brown Jackson." *Politico.* https://www.politico.com/news/magazine/2022/03/21/55-things-you-need-to-know-about-ketanji-brown-jackson-00018514.

Estrada, Miguel. "A Conversation on Judging." Historical Society of the District of Columbia Circuit. YouTube. https://www.youtube.com/watch?v=QuWMeoIAdv8.

Green, Erica L. "At Harvard, a Confederate Flag Spurred Ketanji Brown Jackson to Act." *New York Times.* https://www.nytimes.com/2022/03/20/us/politics/ketanji-brown-jackson-harvard.html?searchResultPosition=16.

Hunter, Natalie. "Ketanji Brown Jackson's Kids: Meet Her Two Daughters, Talia & Leila Jackson." *Hollywood Life.* https://hollywoodlife.com/feature/who-are-ketanji-brown-jackson-kids-4683256/.

Jackson, Ketanji Brown. "35th Edith House Lecture: Ketanji Brown Jackson, U.S. District Court for the District of Columbia." University of Georgia School of Law. YouTube. https://www.youtube.com/watch?v=jXFerWhSckA&t=820s.

"Ketanji Brown Jackson." United States Court of Appeals, District of Columbia Circuit. https://www.cadc.uscourts.gov/internet/home.nsf/content/VL+-+Judges+-+KBJ.

Mazzei, Patricia. "How a High School Debate Team Shaped Ketanji Brown Jackson." *New York Times.* https://www.nytimes.com/2022/02/26/us/ketanji-brown-jackson-high-school-debate.html.

"Miami Hoods to Hoods: Full Tour of Miami Ghetto." *Kulture Vulturez.* https://www.kulturevulturez.com/miami-ghetto-story/.

Mizella, Shawna, and Veronica Stracqualursi. "These are the members of Ketanji Brown Jackson's family." CNN. https://www.cnn.com/2022/03/22/politics/who-is-ketanji-brown-jackson-family/index.html.

Mohl, Raymond A. "On the Edge: Blacks and Hispanics in Metropolitan Miami since 1959." *The Florida Historical Quarterly* 69, no. 1 (1990): 37–56. http://www.jstor.org/stable/30148998.

Morejon, Liane, and Joseph Ojo. "Judge Ketanji Brown Jackson gives a shout out to high school alma matter." *Local 10 News.* https://www.local10.com/news/local/2022/04/08/students-hold-pep-rally-in-celebration-for-judge-ketanji-brown-jackson/.

Niedzwiadek, Nick. "Ketanji Brown Jackson: Who is she? Bio, facts, background and political views." *Politico.* https://www.politico.com/news/2022/02/23/who-is-ketanji-brown-jackson-bio-facts-background-political-views-00010970.

Pilkington, Ed. "Ketanji Brown Jackson's blazing trail to become the first Black female justice." *Guardian.* https://www.theguardian.com/law/2022/apr/07/ketanji-brown-jackson-us-supreme-court-profile.

"President Biden Nominates Judge Ketanji Brown Jackson to Serve as Associate Justice of the U.S. Supreme Court." White House Briefing Room. https://www.whitehouse.gov/briefing-room/statements-releases/2022/02/25/president-biden-nominates-judge-ketanji-brown-jackson-to-serve-as-associate-justice-of-the-u-s-supreme-court/.

"Questionnaire for Judicial Nominees." United States Senate Committee on the Judiciary. https://www.judiciary.senate.gov/imo/media/doc/Jackson%20Senate%20Questionnaire%20Public%20Final.pdf.

"READ: Ketanji Brown Jackson's remarks at the White House after her Supreme Court confirmation." CNN. https://www.cnn.com/2022/04/08/politics/ketanji-brown-jackson-confirmation-speech/index.html.

Roberts, Roxanne. "Ketanji Brown Jackson on being a 'first' and why she loves 'Survivor'." *Washington Post.* https://www.washingtonpost.com/lifestyle/2022/05/16/ketanji-brown-jackson-interview/.

Solomon, Michelle, Christina Vazquez. "Ketanji Brown Jackson's mother grateful for community support." *Local 10 News.* https://www.local10.com/news/local/2022/02/26/ketanji-brown-jacksons-mother-thanks-the-community-for-supporting-her-daughter/.

"The Civil Rights Movement and the Black Experience in Miami." *Miami Libraries Digital Collections.* http://scholar.library.miami.edu/miamiCivilRights/index.html.

For Olympia and Avery,
you can be anything! –D.L.P.

To my mom. The ultimate cheerleader. –K.H.

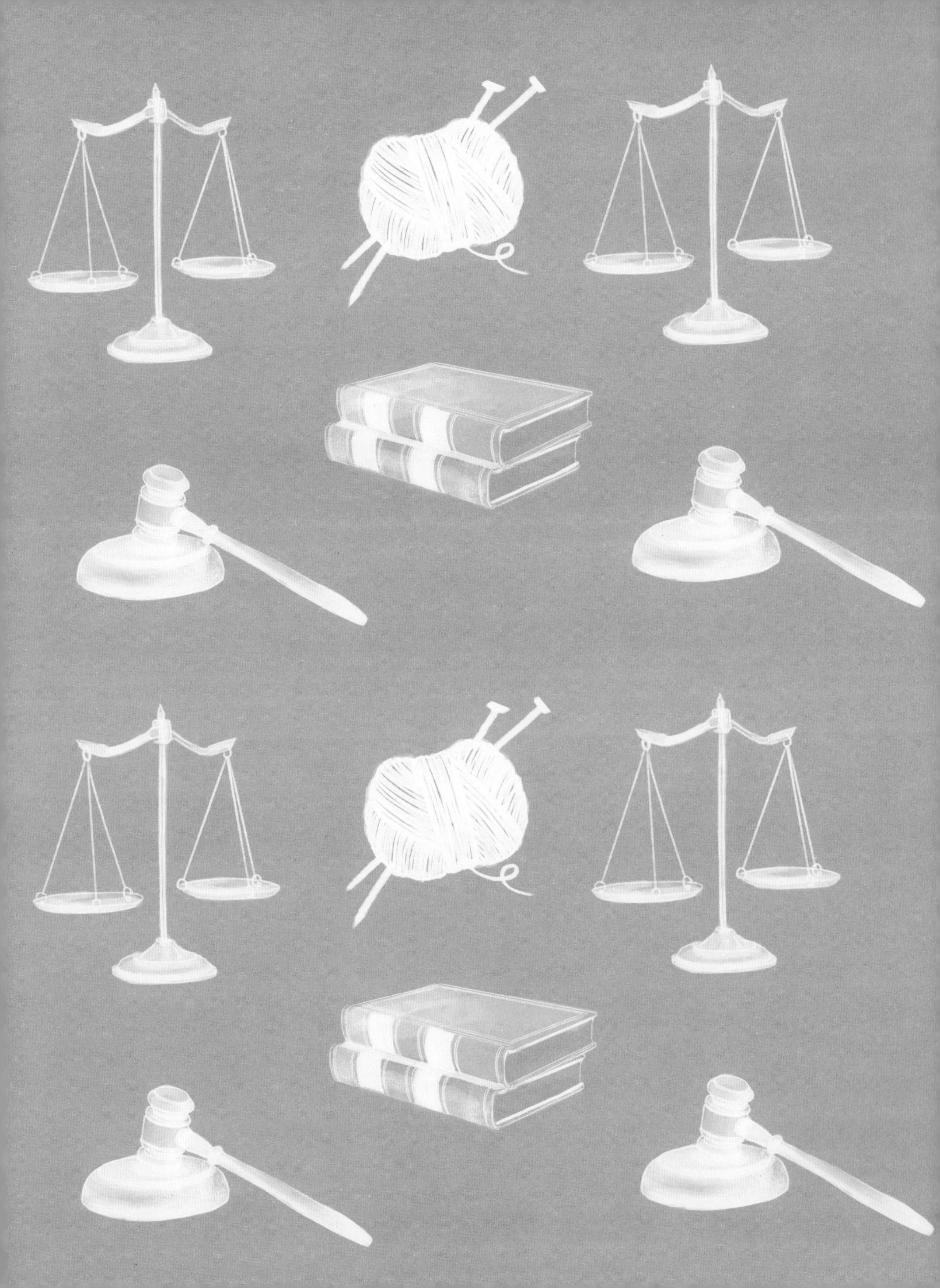